THE ENCHANTED ROAD

HEADCORN MILL

THE
ENCHANTED ROAD

NOT EXACTLY AN EARTHLY STORY WITH A HEAVENLY MEANING,
BUT A TALE OF COMMONPLACE THINGS TOLD WITH THE
ENTHUSIASM OF ONE WHO LOVES THEM MUCH

BY

DONALD MAXWELL

WITH 99 ILLUSTRATIONS

METHUEN & CO. LTD.
36 ESSEX STREET W.C.
LONDON

First Published in 1927

PRINTED IN GREAT BRITAIN

TO MY SKETCH-BOOK

FRIEND of a hundred lonely days,
  Comrade in arms through life's campaign,
Heedless of censure, deaf to praise,
  Nor e'er debased by thoughts of gain ;
A willing slave and swift to obey,
Whether my mood be grave or gay.

What fun we've had : what things we've dared :
  What high adventure have we sought.
What secrets you and I have shared
  In hours the mystic dawn has brought ;
Red riddles of the flaming sky,
Enwrapped in cloudy majesty.

Not yours the style, complete with frame,
  Pleasingly perfect till it palls ;
Not yours the painted picture's fame,
  Flaunted on Piccadilly's walls ;
But modest tints in you combine
With unsophisticated line.

PREFACE

I HAVE spent many days in rambles up and down the country described in this book—the country that lies between London and the heart of the Weald of Kent. I have written of this place and of that place. I have painted from time to time isolated scenes in this zone and I could turn up whole sketch-books of drawings done at all seasons of the year.

One day I conceived the idea of walking from London down into the Weald, linking up these delights in the form of a narrative. I have therefore illustrated this pilgrimage sometimes with fresh sketches and sometimes turning up sketches that I have done before. Consistency has been thrown to the winds, and you may find the seasons somewhat mixed and blossoms or autumn tints occurring in places related as having been seen within ten minutes of each other.

In spite of these vagaries, I have told you a true story, and my most fantastic vision can be vouched for by a surveyor with a plumb line. I have attempted beauty by the selection of what is true rather than by the conscious creation of what is fantastic. Whistler says somewhere that a piano contains all the notes necessary to produce glorious harmony and nature contains all the tones and tints necessary to produce a glorious picture. To tell the artist baldly to go to nature is equivalent to telling the musician to sit on the piano !

Here, then, is an allegory. The Enchanted Road can be found by all who are of good will and keep the hearts of children, but it is hidden from the wise and prudent. There are two roads, the road we must take of necessity and the magic road of our dreams. Sometimes, by some strange alchemy of the mind which some tedious theologians would call the φρόνημα σαρκος and others, more enlightened, would recognize as the Grace of God, the two roads coincide and we are set indeed upon the Enchanted Road.

DONALD MAXWELL

BORSTAL
ROCHESTER
March 25th, 1927

CONTENTS

LIST OF ILLUSTRATIONS

I

The Glamour of The East

LONDON IN FAIRYLAND

WHEN twilight comes to London town,
   If only you will look,
You'll see more wonders than you'll find
   In any picture book.
There are fantasies in Fleet Street
   And castles in the Strand
And magic windows everywhere
   To show you Fairyland.

The fruit-shop round the corner
   Becomes Aladdin's cave :
The lighterman off Pimlico
   Is Sinbad on the wave :
And when the streets are dazzling bright
   And wet with rain, I'm told,
An Alchemist is working hard
   To turn the mud to gold.

O twilight is the magic time
   For deeds of derring do
Goblins are lurking in the squares
   And wicked Ogres, too :
So Knights ride forth in taxicabs
   To rescue maidens fair,
And Dragons out of Charing Cross
   Come snorting from their lair.

    When twilight comes to London town,
      If only you will look,
    You'll see more wonders than you'll find,
      In any picture book.

THE GLAMOUR OF THE EAST

I AWOKE to find a little old man standing at the foot of my bed.

"A happy New Year to you, sir," he began. I replied in suitable terms and asked what I could do for him. He was dressed in a curious way, like a sorcerer out of a fairy-tale book.

"I am a magician by trade," he said and I have brought you a New Year's present—a pair of the very latest magic spectacles. To you, as an artist, they will be invaluable. They will enable you to find Fairyland in the most commonplace scenes of London, to see romance where before you could discern only grim reality. Not only will there be sermons

B

in stones and books in the running brooks : there will be glamour in cement works and poetry in gasometers.

I thanked him most cordially and put them on. As a matter of fact my room looked very much the same as it had done before, but I did not doubt their efficacy.

" These glasses," he went on to explain, " have a latent charm in them.   If you lose them, the situation is not serious, as when you lose ordinary glasses, for when you have once seen through them their power remains in your eyes for ever."

Then we settled down to a long talk about magic and he told me of his experiences in London and the changes he had wrought there from time to time. Many things that had puzzled me concerning London architecture were made as clear as daylight. I have only room to give one instance, but this will be interesting to all who know the City.

" *The enraged magician retaliated by turning a block of offices into a sandwich* "

It appears that my friend the magician, bent on good deeds, one day travelled by train to Cannon Street Station ; but he arrived some minutes after three in the afternoon. Try as he would, he could not get a drink in the refreshment room. The enraged

Down River

magician retaliated by turning a block of offices into a sandwich. They have remained in that condition ever since, so if you doubt the truth of this story you can go there and see them any day.

Suddenly and in the midst of our talk the sorcerer vanished. I was soon up and started off with my sketch-book, on some rather vague intention of setting out on a walking tour. I went first to Cannon Street, and there verified the magician's statement about the sandwich office, and wandered on in an easterly direction. My magic glasses did not show me the buried arch of old London Bridge, but I have been able to turn up a sketch I did when it was discovered in 1920.

The excavation of one of the arches of old London Bridge (built 1176–1209) attracted widespread interest.   Many spoke of it, in the enthusiasm of the moment, as if something lost for many centuries had been discovered, yet it is not so very long ago, as short a time, in fact, as the first year of Queen Victoria's reign, that people were walking over Old London Bridge from Southwark to the City.   The present bridge was begun in 1824 and opened by William IV in 1831.   It crosses the river westward of the old bridge, which likewise was built westward of the one it superseded.   Were excavations to be made on the shores down river probably foundations and traces of successive timber bridges would be found.

The stone arch which the engineers came upon when sinking foundations has been identified as Mill Lock.   The river was not then embanked as it is now, and, consequently, extended at high water to places now hundreds of feet from the water's edge.   This name, Mill Lock, also reminds us that old London Bridge was not only a bridge, but a dam.

Two-thirds of the distance across was occupied with piles or masonry, and there was not time between the tides for a large volume of water to rush out and in again as it does now.   Thus there was a greater depth above the bridge, a boon to small shipping and wharves and a state of things that has often been advocated by engineers of to-day.

I have sketched it here so that its position in relation to the present London

A Thames Tug

Bridge is apparent, some 180
feet to the east, on the City
side of the river.

A " Stumpy "

Another link with the
past and the good old days
is Execution Dock, at
Wapping. Certain alterations
by Wapping Old Stairs had
been rumoured. I hurried
down to Wapping, sketch-book in hand, before it was too late,
but could not find anything reminiscent of " Treasure Island "
or Captain Kidd, the bold, bad buccaneer, who was hanged
here after a long run for his money. The local watermen
point out a quay (it shows at right of sketch on page 13)
as the site of this notorious place. The stairs themselves, as
will be seen from the drawing, are rather picturesque amid
their drab and prosaic surroundings. It will be noticed that
there are really two flights of stairs. That on the left, the
narrower of the two, which leads up to a garden door and is
in a state of ruinous disrepair, is sometimes pointed out as
being stairs up which Captain Kidd and other pirates of the
old days walked to their doom.

History did not seem to be the strong point of the riverside
denizens of Wapping—they have other things to attend to—
but in the course of peregrinations I came across two small
boys in a boat who made up for all omissions by telling me
lurid stories of pirates tied up and drowned by the rising
tide at this very spot, and of rusty swords which, as they
asserted, their grandfathers had found in a hole in the wall
hard by.

I was soon at Wapping Old Stairs, hard by which historic landing are the headquarters of the Thames Police. I do not know whether or not my new spectacles influenced my sight, but this bit of shore with its post and floating stage seemed to me to be reminiscent of Venice—Venice in a key of black and grey. I went into the Station and here found one or two old friends—for the captain of the good ship *Penguin* is well known to the police.

Of the work of the police in London we are bound to see a good deal. The control of traffic in the streets, to take only one example, keeps the efficiency of the force constantly before us. We are beginning to hear something of the activities of women police and are getting quite used to these uniformed Amazons in various London centres : but of the organization of the River Police and their most important and often dangerous work in patrolling the miles of London's

Below the Pool

waterway, with its im-
mense wealth of goods
in ship and barge and
lighter, we hear very
little and indeed see
very little, for, in the
very nature of things, it
is not very conspicuous
work when viewed from
the shore.

Three men in a boat

The only river police
activities noticeable to
the average Londoner are the motor-boats coming alongside
or leaving the police pier on the Embankment at Waterloo
Bridge, and an occasional glimpse of three men in a boat,
that is, three policemen in a motor-boat, visible from one
of the bridges. Yet the Thames and everything afloat upon
it are on their beat, which extends from Teddington Lock to
Dartford.

A good deal was written some time ago about a reign of
terror on the Thames. Barges are said to have been broken
into and lighters so frequently robbed that insurance com-
panies have refused in some cases to cover the risk of loss.
It would appear, however, from various inquiries that I
made at the time, there was a good deal of exaggeration.

The very uncertainty of the movements of these little
police boats amongst the anchored ships and moored hosts
of lighters is a strong deterrent to potential evil-doers.
At any moment a motor-boat with her three blue-uniformed
occupants may pop round the corner. When any pilferer

or river bandit is caught red-handed and arrested he is taken to the river police station at Wapping or Waterloo and charged there. Only in the case of a capture being made at a long distance from one of these stations is the prisoner handed over to the custody of the ever-vigilant police on shore.

The patrols of the motor-boats, each with its three men, are divided into eight-hour spells. There are generally about twenty-four boats in use between Teddington and Dartford, consequently a keen eye is kept on all movements on the river. The " characters " of most of the users of boats are well known to the police, and he would be a smart man who could systematically unload lighters and barges and get the stuff away without their knowledge. The safety of the lonely reaches of the river, it may be added, is largely in the hands of the very energetic and efficient watch on the Thames.

Soon I am at Blackwall and at the gates of the Trinity House quays at Blackwall. To those that go down to the sea in ships or have business in great waters—and I suppose if there are any " great " waters around our coasts they are those upon the road to London—then Trinity House looms large. A word therefore on the subject.

A small vessel making her way from a British port, we will say Great Yarmouth, and proceeding to Oxford, would pass through three separate aquatic kingdoms. The first would be what I have described as the Realm of Trinity House, for that ancient corporation is responsible for the placing and maintaining of buoys, lightships, lighthouses and beacons to mark channels by day and light the coast at night and the River Thames as far up as London Bridge.

"LONDON BRIDGE IS BROKEN DOWN"

EXCAVATION OF AN OLD ARCH AND ITS POSITION
IN RELATION TO THE PRESENT BRIDGE

NEAR EXECUTION DOCK, WAPPING

Here it, for purposes of lighting, overlaps the second kingdom, the Port of London Authority. At a point just below Teddington Lock the third kingdom begins, the Thames Conservancy, and extends for the whole course of the river and of its tributary streams.

In describing Trinity House, I should seek to be brief with my written notes, leaving a maximum of room for my pencil, but I am prevented at the outset by having to give the full name of the Trinity House organization, and this itself takes up whole inches of room. Hereinafter called Trinity House, the governing body is an association of mariners founded in the reign of Henry VIII, and legally styled *The Masters, Wardens and Assistants of the Guild, Fraternity or Brotherhood of the Most Glorious and Undivided Trinity and of St. Clement in the Parish of Deptford Strond— commonly called the Corporation of Trinity House of Deptford Strond* and, we might add to this, *spoken of to-day as Trinity House.*

For many centuries the keeping up of lighthouses and beacons was a matter of private enterprise or pious monastic labour. Sometimes it would be a mild kind of blackmail, for the owner of a lighthouse was empowered to collect toll from passing ships. The Corporation of Trinity House gradually became responsible for an efficient system of buoyage and lighting, but there was no uniformity of ownership. In the reign of George IV, however, full power and monopoly was given to Trinity House, and all private lighthouses were bought up.

The edifice which gives the present name to the Brotherhood is the venerable Trinity House, in Trinity Square, by

the Tower.   Its stately rooms and its Reynolds's portraits
are alone worth a visit.   But the quays at Blackwall are still
more intriguing to me, a unique region where avenues of
buoys, like stranded sea monsters, give vistas of shipping
in the busy Thames.

It is a strange place, at the mouth of the River Lea, with
a square-faced house painted battleship-grey, with experi-
mental lighthouses and an occasional spare lightship.   Every
lightship and buoy must have a duplicate ready at any time
in case of accident.   Buoys are often carried away and
lightships damaged, and if these are not replaced at once
navigation is fraught with great danger.

It is in thick weather and in the obscurity of night that
the mariner picks up his safe course along a well-buoyed or
well-lighted channel and calls down blessings upon the Masters,
Wardens and Assistants of the Guild, Fraternity or Brotherhood of the Most Glorious and Undivided Trinity and of St.
Clement in the Parish of Deptford Strond—commonly called
the Corporation of Trinity House of Deptford Strond.

The history of London and its growth from the Middle
Ages until to-day is largely the history and growth of shipping.
In the Middle Ages, when few craft could have been larger
than 100 tons, the quays of the City were few indeed—those
of the Fleet River, Billingsgate, Queenhithe and Dowgate—
vessels for the most part lying in the stream and discharging
into boats and lighters.   With the building of a stone bridge
across the river in 1209 wharves sprang up on the Southwark
side.   Before this event the prospect of being cut off from easy
communication with the City in case of fire—a fear justified
by experience—had kept warehouses and quays to the north

A LANDING STAGE BY THE RIVER
POLICE STATION AT WAPPING

shore alone. Nevertheless, making full use of all the facilities the port could offer, the steady growth of shipping always overcrowded the quays, and the very success of London as a place for the handling of ship-borne goods rendered congestion inevitable.

In 1705 agitation for reform had grown to considerable proportions. Traders banded themselves together and demanded that Parliament should pay serious attention to the matter. They pointed to Bristol as the example of a much smaller place which had greater facilities for shipping. Whereas the great port of London had only 1,400 feet of quays, Bristol had 4,000.

Parliament, like many Parliaments since, promised that something should be done, that an inquiry would be held. History does not record what happened at the inquiry.

There was one dock in use at Rotherhithe soon after 1700. Deptford at this time was a Naval Dockyard, and a dock was made on the south side of the river, becoming, with various later additions, the Surrey Commercial Docks. The private venture of a Mr. Perry in 1789 was the construction of a basin for the use of the ships of the East India Company.

The state of the riverside, with its " pirates," " night plunderers," " scuffle hunters " and the like, was unbearable, enormous losses falling upon traders. A meeting of public bodies in 1799 carried certain resolutions, finally petitioning Parliament. The upshot of this action was the passing of the two Dock Bills and an acceptance of the docks system as the best method that could be adopted for improving the Port of London.

The West India Dock Act, 1799, was followed by the London Dock Act in the next year and the East India Dock Act four years after. St. Katharine's Dock Bill passed in 1824, and Millwall Dock saw the light in 1868. The Act authorizing the Royal Albert Dock, with the extension of which we are now concerned, was passed in 1875, followed hard by the Tilbury Dock scheme in 1882. Thus it was that the great dock system of the Port of London came into being.

In 1921 a large new dock was opened by the King, who journeyed thither by water. The importance of this addition is emphasized by the Port of London Authority's statement that now ships up to 30,000 tons can be berthed within 6½ miles of the City, whereas hitherto a very big ship could be accommodated only at Tilbury, and there a vessel of 19,000 tons was the largest that could enter.

*The curious scenery of the quays
at the mouth of the River Lea*

Off Greenwich

The entrance lock is 800 feet long and 100 feet wide, with a depth of 45 feet below Trinity high-water, and by means of a floating caisson at the inner end a total length of 910 feet can be obtained. A dry dock, which can be seen in the lower sketch at the far end of the new basin, will take a ship 750 feet long, and an army of twenty-four 3-ton electric level-luffing cranes, shown above, makes a formidable array along the North Quay, where three double-story sheds of great capacity have been built.

The main dock works, which were commenced in 1912, were arrested by the war, but were continued in 1918, and the improvement has been completed at a total cost of £4,500,000. The water area is 64 acres, the depth is 38 feet, and the surrounding quay walls are 10,000 feet long, providing fourteen berths for steamers of the largest size.

TRINITY HOUSE QUAY,
BLACKWALL

THE SPECIALISTS

Blackwall Reach is sloppy and wet
  —Water the colour of mud—
And fifty barges are thrashing up
  For the wind's against the flood :
Port and starboard, starb'd and port
  By collier, schooner and tramp ;
" Greenwich is nigh and our throats are dry
  But everything else is damp."

The *Elizabeth Ann* is the foremost sail,
  Her skipper, he points to a dome :
" My friend the Astronomer Royal," he says,
  " Lives there in his onion home.
But 'ow he calculates the tide
  And writes about the weather,
Gettin' the fac's for the halmanacks,
  —It beats me altogether."

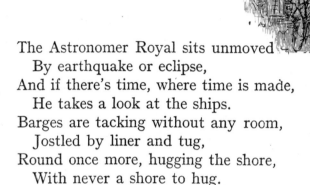

The Astronomer Royal sits unmoved
   By earthquake or eclipse,
And if there's time, where time is made,
   He takes a look at the ships.
Barges are tacking without any room,
   Jostled by liner and tug,
Round once more, hugging the shore,
   With never a shore to hug.

The Astronomer Royal gazes down
   At the dodging *Elizabeth Ann.*
" Her skipper," he says, " has hardly the cut
   Of a mathematical man.
   And **how** he calculates the tide
   And steers in foggy weather,
And how he can learn just where to turn
   —It beats me altogether."

GREENWICH OBSERVATORY

THE ROAD BENEATH THE RIVER.

BLACK MAGIC

RETRACING my steps until again I came to the place where the road plunges downwards, the traveller in search of the Kentish shore passes under the river. An avenue of lights, reflected in fantastic curves upon the glazed white surface of the tunnel, lead on to the dim distance, suggesting that the destination of all this clanging and roaring traffic was somewhere in the centre of the earth. The din is deafening and indescribable and there is a touch of black magic about this sub-fluvian roadway and it seems an endless road.

On emerging upon the other side of the river I made friends with a man in the gas works and climbed to some considerable height upon a gasometer, from which point of vantage can be seen the river and the entrance to the tunnel in the same view. I sketched the scene in colour, but it has in some inexplicable way been lost, so I cannot reproduce it here. It could not, however, more than suggest the fantastic and eerie effect of the moving streams of men and vehicles descending into the nether regions, while above them surge the tides, to and fro, upon the river-road of London.

I once happened to journey through this tunnel very early in the morning. The night had been misty and when I emerged on the Kentish side of the river I found the world lit by a pale green light. I had not gone three hundred yards when I chanced to look back and saw high in the sky a strange tracery in blue, stretched across a background of amber and grey. A moment's observation told me that the tracery was made by gasometers, the bases of which were lost in haze.

The scene was of great delicacy and charm. The colour of it all I cannot show you, but I have put down here some semblance of its form. There is a moral, too, in all this. Look for beauty always and everywhere and you may find it in the most unlikely places.

Not a few of my friends and acquaintances have taken me to task for this enjoyment of beauty in the midst of squalor, and they foresee a great danger of fostering the toleration of dreadful conditions of human life and of industrial work. If these things are idealized, they say, instead of abolished we shall not get on very fast with the building of Jerusalem in England's green and pleasant land.

The objection is one that will not bear examination. In the first place the danger of employers of labour observing the effects of sunset in their works instead of looking after

" The tracery was made by gasometers, the bases of which were lost in haze "

the material condition of the place—well, it is a very remote danger. Moreover, the only people who are likely to see beauty in gasometers and sublimity in chimneys are those very people who are building the new world, for they alone have imagination and without imagination nothing creative is done at all.

The faculty of being able to idealize is like a sense of humour—necessary and salutary in an imperfect world but in a state of material or moral perfection would become as redundant as antidotes in a world without poisons.

Apart from idealization and poetry there is generally something of fitness and even of beauty in a thing that has been made for use if that use is adequately fulfilled—or should it be said in the degree in which it is adequately fulfilled. The first steam engine, the first motor car, and the first steamboat did not develop into lines of shapeliness until the usefulness had been alone made the standard of workmanship. Then they became things which fitted their environment.

Now that I was on the south side of the river I went towards the Surrey Docks and struck one of the most curious waterways in London. It is familiar to people who travel through Rochester to Charing Cross, but I have never met anyone who really knew anything about it—whence it comes from and whither it goes. The reason is not far to seek. It goes to nowhere. At one time, when canal schemes were in the air, there may have been some idea of linking up the Surrey Docks with places South of London on a scale more ambitious than that achieved. At present the canal ends ignominiously near Peckham Rye about two miles only from its beginning.

There is one spot in particular that I wished to find because I have seen it so often from the train. It is seen from the right hand side as the train approaches London.

"THERE WAS AN ALCHEMIST,
AS LARGE AS LIFE, TURNING
BLACK TAR INTO GOLD"

" THE BIG DOME THAT LOOMS GREY,
DIMLY DISCERNED AGAINST THE
STAR-SPANGLED SKY "

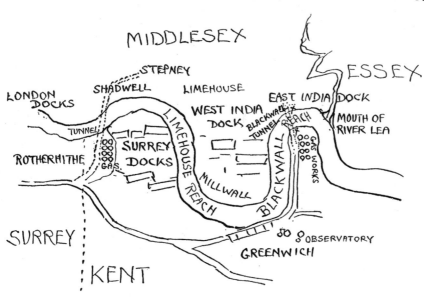

On one bank is a fore-shore that is always strewn with an imposing litter of barrels and jars and on the other is some kind of a distillery (I think, as a matter of fact, it is a varnish factory) with most exciting little domes with pipes leading out of them, mysteriously used long ago, I am sure, by some alchemist of the middle ages but now put to more directly commercial purposes.

I found the place at last and I was delighted to find that my guess had been right. There sure enough were strange cauldrons and diabolical retorts and there was an alchemist, as large as life, turning black tar into gold. He was mounted on a short ladder and looking into an enormous pot, suitable for boiling oxen whole. I could not see quite how he was transmuting the tar, but I caught him in the act and my

sketch, which is " not less than truth designed," is evidence
if you should doubt my story.

Besides I have other evidence that black magic is prac-
tised on the Surrey Canal.   As I was sketching the manager
of the works came out to see what I was doing.   He was most
interested and I asked him point blank :

" Tell me, am I not right in describing that old man on
the ladder as one who is transmuting black tar into gold."

" You are perfectly right," he replied, " although I have
never heard it put in quite that way before.   The by-products
of tar are a gold mine if studied scientifically "—then he went
off into technicalities which do not concern us.

But you will agree, that the manager of the works would
know his own alchemist—so I am right and my story is quite
true, and so I left the Surrey Canal well pleased with my discovery and entered into Greenwich Park.

It is very fortunate that the enjoyment of many things is
independent of technical knowledge.   We can be enthralled
by music without having any notion of counterpoint.   We
can revel in the beauty of a picture without the vaguest idea
as to the nature of egg-tempera or the technique of oil painting ; and we can set our watches, take the time of the tide,
and gaze with awe upon the many-domed Observatory at
Greenwich without much understanding of the accumulation
of astronomical knowledge necessary to furnish us with
material.

In accord with this fortunate circumstance, and in a spirit
of happy ignorance, I approached Greenwich Observatory and
wandered round and about the strange buildings set upon
the crest of the rising ground.   From One Tree Hill, the spot

MORDEN COLLEGE, BLACKHEATH

from which the sketch at the top of page 28 is taken, they appear to form a miniature Jerusalem, as seen from Mount Scopus.

By night the mystery of the place is enhanced, and the domes and towers as they rise in dark silhouette again remind us somewhat of the East, especially the big dome that looms grey, as seen from one of the gardens of the Observatory, dimly discerned against the star-spangled sky.

I should like to know the meaning of many things that I can see against the skyline—strange instruments for reading the riddle of the stars.   No doubt if I called at the Observatory and asked, all these mysteries would be courteously explained.

I am afraid of spoiling the illusion.   I like to think of the astronomers within as dignified old men, with long white beards and black skull-caps, gazing into the inter-stellar spaces of the heavens throughout the long watches of the silent night.   Perhaps they would not be of this type in reality, and the " close-up " would weaken the suggestion of mystery.

That this ignorance of the details of the astronomer's life is shared by others was revealed to me one day in a rather amusing manner.   A nurse arrived with two children, the latter evidently finding the Observatory a novelty and gazing at it in some awe.

" Nanny," said one, " where are the astronomers ? " " Sssh ! " replied the nurse, " they are all asleep."   The significance of the remark did not strike me at once.   Doubtless the astronomers, being up all night looking at the stars through their telescopes, would be resting during the hours of daylight.

Leaving the Observatory and Greenwich Park by the gate leading to Blackheath I am constrained to linger at that haunt of ancient peace, Morden College, a home for merchants of London who, through no fault of their own, have come to need a pension. The founder, a silk merchant of London, lost all his money by the loss of some ships in the East.

He suffered great want and misfortune, when it turned out that the news of the wrecking of his ships was false and that pirates had captured them and were trading with them. After some time these vessels were regained and the good fortune of the owner became established. He was so impressed with the need of some fund for merchants who by like misfortune should require assistance that he founded this delightful retreat.

In the grounds at the back of this old building are twelve elm trees, known as the twelve apostles. I have sketched this view because it is just here that a new road (projected) threatens to turn this haunt of ancient peace into a pandemonium of noisy motors, although the building itself is not in danger of destruction.

As this part of the enchanted road concerns black magic and fairy-land generally I am bent on discovering the dragon's castle and so come to Shooter's Hill and sketch it on page 46, facing it with an appropriate contrast.

Perhaps as illustrations to a fairy tale—a fairy tale that can be realized by the most hum-drum worker of London— the subjects would fit in better. There is the dragon's castle, and then we wander on until we come suddenly to a dear little cottage in the wood, and all sorts of things might happen. Castle Wood, a delightful little coppice clinging to the side of

The Lake, Danson Park

the hill that slopes sharply away to Eltham and Well Hall, contains an architectural curiosity that is worth a visit.

This is the tower referred to, known as Severndroog Castle, which was built by Lady James to commemorate the taking of a fort of this name on the coast of Malabar by her husband, Sir William James, a distinguished soldier in the service of the East India Company, in 1755. This curious structure is said—with what truth I cannot say—to be a replica of one of the forts of Severndroog, which thus fell into British hands. Over the main doorway of the edifice a stone tablet has been inserted in the wall setting out briefly the history of the building. It is in the following terms :

This building was erected MDCCLXXXIV by the representatives of the late

Sir William James, Bart.,

to commemorate that gallant officer's achievement in the East Indies during his command of the Company's Marine Forces in those seas ; and in particular to record the conquest of the Castle of Severndroog, on the coast of

Malabar, which fell to his superior valour and able conduct on the 2nd day of April, MDCCLV.

The drawing of this cottage and the subject *facing* it of Severndroog Castle are of places some miles apart. The arrangement of these two sketches almost tempts me to sing—

> The rich man in his castle,
> The poor man at his gate—

to quote from that hymn which so enrages Communists, but for the fact that the label will not fit. The real fact, of course, under the new order of things, is that in this case the castle will be the poor man's, which can be reached from London for a twopenny fare on a London County Council tram, and the cottage will hardly be that of a poor man, within the poet's meaning, inasmuch as it may be assumed that a keeper of such a delightful spot as Danson Park will have an adequately paid and congenial job.

The house that once stood in these grounds has been pulled down—it was not a very beautiful building, and it was not much loss—and in its place there have been laid out some very delightful terrace gardens, which are a distinct advantage to the place. The view from these gardens is extensive, and includes all that valley lying to the south of the hill, with a foreground of woodland. These woods, known as Jack's Wood, have also been taken over and most sensibly left in their wild state. Very delightful are they to wander in, with their fine old trees and soft carpet of leafy turf.

SEVERNDROOG CASTLE

THE COTTAGE IN THE WOOD

Both the Severndroog Estate and Jack's Wood have been taken over by the L.C.C., and the two places certainly form a pleasant oasis in the rather uninteresting country round about Woolwich, much of which, especially towards Well Hall, is still covered with serried ranks of wooden huts—ugly relics of war-time days—that are anything but dignified as permanent memorials of the housing controversy.

Danson Park, Welling, has been recently added to the pastures new of outer London, Councillor Savage and his workers on the Bexley Urban District Council being the heroes of the hour. When this fine estate came into the market, instead of allowing it to fall into the hands of the builders, as so many estates round London inevitably do, they decided to buy it for the people of Bexley. For this generous act these people, and many others who visit here, should be for ever grateful, for Danson Park is certainly a fair prospect. Undulating parkland, well-laid-out gardens, and the magnificent lake of over twenty acres will form a " playground " within easy reach of London.

The lake is a wonderful sheet of water and one of the longest in Kent—to look at from the house it appears like a river. Each end is hidden in the trees, and it is dotted with small wooded islands, where wild ducks and herons have their nests. Other wild-fowl are much in evidence here, and it is to be hoped that they will continue to remain and not be driven away by the merry crowds that will throng thither.

When I went over this estate just before it was thrown open to the public an official told me that the small ponds at the head of this lake were mentioned in the old documents as *Store Ponds*. He judged that they were for storing water for the lake! I should be rather inclined to guess that if the word is store, it was used in connexion with storing fish. Possibly it is a corruption of Stew Pond, which is a name often found in this connexion.

In Danson Park

III
There Go The Ships

OVER THE MARSHES

OVER the marshes down our way
   There's lots of things to see,
And if you are passing our farm one day
   You can come with Sissy and me.
We climb on a gate—its awf'ly high,
   But Sissy gives me a hand—
And we watch the ships go sailing, sailing,
   Sailing over the land.

One ship was going abroad, I'm told,
   Where everyone's inky black,
And once I waved to the captain bold,
   But the captain didn't wave back.
His ship had balconies round the top
   It looked so big and grand :
And I watched it sailing, sailing, sailing,
   Sailing over the land.

At night there comes a fairy town
   And magic lamps peep out
And lights go creeping up and down
   Like stars that walk about.
We see them over uncle's field,
   Stretched like a diamond band,
And we know the ships are sailing, sailing,
   Sailing over the land.

Sometimes my mummie keeps me in
   Because I've got a chill :
And once I didn't get up for a week,
   When I was prop'ly ill :
But the steamers hooted to me in bed
   For they knew I'd understand,
That still they were sailing, sailing, sailing,
   Sailing over the land.

THERE GO THE SHIPS

ALTHOUGH aiming at Bexley my course had been rather like that of a merchant vessel proceeding in submarine-infested waters. A detour from Bexley brought me down to Abbey Wood and on to the swamp levels, for I had heard of a place named Crossness upon the river and was curious to see what it had to offer in the way of riverside scenery. That this would not be much was abundantly evident, but I was not prepared for such utter blankness. The road ran across a melancholy marsh on which stood a dead tree and a dismal black building. The heights of Bostall Wood, though pleasant in themselves, seemed to throw this plain into still deeper desolation. Then the track came to the river's bank, a place of Stygian foulness, where the shattered and decayed posts of some vast but vanished landing-stage were performing a dance of death.

A more depressing region I have seldom seen, and I shook this mud from off my feet and came into Abbey Wood again, to find the curious hollow by the Abbey site which is still pointed out as a place of shipbuilding. There is nothing left of the abbey but a wall, and the hollow which once rang with hammers and the songs of the shipwrights at work upon wooden walls would need the keen eye of a topographical detective to see it, were it not for tradition. It stands at a bend in the road (the road with the tram-lines) west of Belvedere Station. Below is the nomadic settlement of the gipsies, a township of caravans, some of them gaily painted and others in the last stage of patchwork decay.

Regaining the long and dreary road at Bexley Heath, I found great relief in descending upon Bexley and following the lower road by the pleasant River Cray. I had entered Arcady at last, and the leafy stillness was restful. I found for the first time an old white mill which I had so often seen from the train but never reached by road, and I found, what

A melancholy marsh,
by Abbey Wood

The ghost of a pier at Crossness

to me was a discovery, the delightful haunt of ancient peace, Hall Place. I suppose all architects and antiquaries know all about it, but it came as a great revelation to me to what extent panelled flint was used in old time. There are numerous examples of chequered black and white made by alternating flints and hewn stone, but Hall Place is (the old part) entirely built in chequers. My sketch of it was made from across the stream. The chequered work, however, can be best seen from the road.

And so through Dartford to Gravesend, where I took the path along the Gravesend-Rochester canal. It is a delightful walk, possessing a strange fascination, for from here the ships seem to be sailing over the land.

Before the advent of the railway there were in England

great schemes afoot for canalizing various links between river systems. One of these materialized in the form of the short cut from the Thames at Gravesend to the Medway at Rochester—a distance of about eight miles, instead of about forty via Sheerness. At Higham the canal pierced the hills by means of a tunnel, and, some two miles farther on, emerged at Strood.

The railway came, bought up the canal, which still exists as far as Higham, and then ran trains through the tunnel, the waterway being filled up. The spectacle can sometimes be seen, as in this picture, of a barge, train and aeroplane

" And the hollow which once rang with hammers and the songs of the shipwrights at work upon wooden walls "

(Abbey Wood)

Hall Place, Bexley

(dimly seen, left top corner) all travelling together, a striking instance of " milestones " in transport history.

The canal of 1844 was not a financial success because, owing to difficulties of tide levels at each end, a barge passing through was not able to get out again as soon as she had made the seven-mile voyage. Thus, if there was any wind, barges could often sail round via Sheerness and be up at Strood as soon as through the canal, incidentally saving dues.

However, there was a good deal of use made of it by the Maidstone barges.

The South Eastern Railway bought up the canal. The towpath was broadened by carrying out a platform on piles, and on that a single line was laid.

At a later date what remained of the waterway was filled in and a double line run through the tunnel.

It has always been a source of wonder to me that artists —including myself—have not made more of trains as subjects or accessories in pictures. Like all new mechanical devices, the first examples were ugly. The first steamboat, the first motor-car, and the first aeroplane were all makeshift-looking things, for no evolution had set in to modify the type, and, by a survival of the fittest, conform its lines to a real expression of its use and of its environment. In the case, for instance, of a railway carriage, still retaining its old name of " coach," the designers went on building ordinary coaches, putting them upon iron wheels that ran on lines, but otherwise keeping the essentials of a road vehicle long after its main characteristics had become meaningless and obsolete —even to the piling of baggage on the top of the carriage in which its owners travelled. The very term booking-office is a relic of the days when the passengers entered their names in a book to secure their place in the coach.

The first motor-cars were silly-looking things, the complete absence of a horse in front of the splash-board and whip-socket being their most noticeable feature. Both train and car have evolved into shapely and expressive objects, and the distant train, with its white smoke-pennant across the green Weald of Kent, and the touring car climbing the

THE OLD ROCHESTER-GRAVESEND CANAL

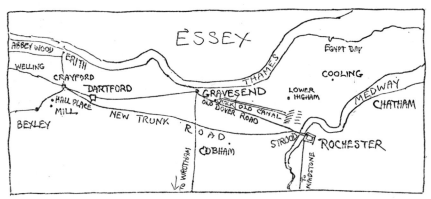

Bexley to Rochester

steep highways of the Downs, take their place in the landscape as naturally as the old-time windmill or the galloping
horseman.

It is now a hundred years since a group of men, of whom
one was George Stephenson, experimented and invented the
locomotive.

In 1825 Stephenson drove an engine with thirty-four
trucks, thus demonstrating its utility. Five years after-
wards the first railway was opened and the great transport
revolution was an accomplished fact.

Perhaps now that railways are as much a feature of our
age as windmills were in the age of Rembrandt, some painter
will make a classic of " The Train " as Rembrandt did of
" The Mill."

Turner lived too soon to do it. When he painted his
" Rain, Steam, and Speed : The Great Western Railway,"
trains were looked upon as marvels and curiosities. Artists

drew them, when they drew them at all, as we drew the first aeroplanes. It was sufficiently exciting to see that a man was flying. The wonder was that he was in the air instead of on the ground; anything could symbolize the aeroplane —a few struts and planes and the thing was done. No one could mistake it for a barge or a bird.

It was in this spirit that Turner saw the engine in " Rain, Steam, and Speed." Here was a strange thing, a boiler with fire and cinders, a smoky monster that could go nearly as fast as a hare, a portent, a prophecy, a revolution that would sweep away the old order of things. Horses might still be used for ploughing—even that is rather a hazy idea; but steam now rules the world. The sea is already conquered. The fighting *Temeraire* moved proudly to her last berth to the spluttering and splashing of a fussy tug, for the old order has given way to the new, and now the land, as well as the sea, has been brought under the iron dominion of steam.

As it was in such a mood that Turner pictured a Great Western engine, it is no good looking for a historical record from the point of view of the engineer. Had the painter lived to-day he would, no doubt, have found the railways of England a fruitful field for picture making.

This is the land of Great Expectations, and before I get to the end of this canal, where it becomes railway alone, Lower Higham comes into sight. This has been finally identified as Our Village by Colonel Gadd, who has given a sort of ex cathedra pronouncement on the subject accepted by most Dickensians because of the obvious reason that it alone fits the references in the book. Various claimants—

THE WHITE MILL AT BEXLEY

Cooling and Chalk being the favourites—have been disposed of.

The fact that the tombs in Cooling Churchyard have been put into the picture and Joe Gargery's forge at Chalk taken as a model and exactly described has given colour to each of these villages being possible originals, but the main point and plot of the story would be invalidated if either of these was Our Village. The isolation of the church from the village—distant about a mile—is the pivot on which the early part of the book turns, and the fact that the convict is described as crossing a muddy creek stepping from stone to stone. This would be possible at Cooling, but Cooling Church is not isolated from the village. Chalk Church is a long way from the village, but it is high on the hill.

In Lower Higham this creek (before the railway was made) came right up to the church wall. There was a ferry-house, a farm, and possibly two cottages in the neighbourhood. This is called Church Street and is a mile from the village of Lower Higham. My sketch on page 67 shows Church Street, and the one on page 69 the gate by the church through which the soldiers went with their sergeant on the Christmas Day hunt for the convict. The hulks—vessels like Noah's Arks —were on the river across the marshes, probably in Egypt Bay.

Then follows a word-picture which is one of the best landscapes I know.

" The marshes were just a long black horizontal line then, as I stopped to look after him ; and the river was just another horizontal line, not nearly so broad nor yet so black ; and the sky was just a row of long angry red lines and dense

black lines intermixed.   On the edge of the river I could
faintly make out the only two black things in all the prospect
that seemed to be standing upright ; one of these was the
beacon by which the sailors steered—like an unhooped cask
upon a pole—an ugly thing when you were near it ; the
other, a gibbet, with some chains hanging to it which had
once held a pirate."

The marshes below Gravesend

It would be idle to look for these old poles and beacons
now, but the gaunt light standing on legs upon the sea
wall by Lower Higham is sufficiently characteristic to
illustrate this passage. I have made a rough sketch of this
above.

Church Street, Lower Higham

At the end of this chapter I have made a rough sketch of the general appearance of the tombstone and " lozenges " at Cooling, used by Dickens as a model for the " scenery " of the opening chapter of *Great Expectations*.

" I give Pirrip as my father's family name, on the authority of his tombstone and my sister—Mrs. Joe Gargery, who married the blacksmith. As I never saw my father or my mother, and never saw any likeness of either of them (for their days were long before the days of photographs), my first fancies regarding what they were like, were unreasonably derived from their tombstones. The shape of the letters on my father's, gave me an odd idea that he was a square, stout, dark man, with curly black hair. From the character and turn of the inscription, ' *also Georgiana Wife of the Above*,' I drew a childish conclusion that my mother was freckled and sickly. To five little stone lozenges, each about a foot and a half long, which were arranged in a neat row beside their grave, and were sacred to the memory of five little brothers of mine—who gave up trying to get a living exceedingly early

A buttressed cottage at the Higham end of the canal

in that universal struggle—I am indebted for a belief I religiously entertained that they had all been born on their

Lower Higham Church and the marshes. The scene of the Christmas Day convict hunt in " Great Expectations "
—" then we struck out on the open marshes, through the gate at the side of the churchyard "

backs with their hands in their trouser-pockets, and had never taken them out in this state of existence."

By the time I had finished all the examination of Lower

Higham the light had gone and my best road into Rochester was by train through the tunnel, which, as we have seen, was once the barge route linking the Thames with the Medway.

Tombstones in Cooling Churchyard

IV

The Road Through Rochester

E

ROCHESTER CITY

ROCHESTER CITY, U.S.A.,
  Is a very fine place, I'm told,
The houses are high and the streets are straight
And everything in them is up to date
And everything's made of gold.
  America loves to set the way
In a land that is dry—and free ;
But as for Rochester, U.S.A.—
Well, I've never been there to see !

There's another Rochester down in Kent,
And, that I know full well ;
There's mud in the water and smoke in the air
And a profitless castle all out of repair,
And a sort of cementy smell ;
  And the street where the traffic's jammed all day
Was old when Cæsar came.
It hasn't got much of the Yankee touch,
But we love it, all the same.

And when I am travelling far from home,
With Arabs to pitch my tent,
The Medway shines as the sun declines
And I study the walls of Babylon's shrines,
Because they suggest cement.
  And when the rush of the monsoon rain
Re-echoes from Delhi ridge,
I can hear once more the rumble and roar
Of a train upon Rochester Bridge.

Rochester Castle and Bridge

THE ROAD THROUGH ROCHESTER

IT is a strange thing, now that I come to reflect upon it, that so many people who have passed through Rochester by train, and who are otherwise unacquainted with it, should be impressed by the idea that Rochester and the country round about it is flat. This impression is the more remarkable when it is remembered that the railway lines to Rochester from both Gravesend and Chatham are through tunnels and from Victoria by means of the most formidable gradient in the south of England. It is possible to enter Rochester by train only from the direction of Maidstone without noticing the hilly nature of the country, so we are driven to the conclusion that all these " flat Rochester people " are either

very unobservant or that they come from Maidstone at night
or when the weather is misty.

However, a traveller stepping from the train at Rochester
Station (assuming that he has been asleep and noticed neither
gradient nor tunnel) would readily agree, from what he saw,
that this was no land for mountaineering. The creeks and
saltings close at hand, more creeks and saltings across the
water, and, beyond the chimneys and cement quays, an
almost limitless vista of still more creeks and saltings and
the level expanse of busy Dockyard Land in the distance—
all these would tend to strengthen the hypothesis that
Rochester must indeed be flat.

If the tide is up, there will be water almost to the station
and the platform will seem like the deck of a ship. There
will probably be vessels loading or unloading close at hand,
and, whatever else is missing, there will be plenty of barges
—barges aground, barges under sail, barges moored in com-
panies, lonely barges, barges with brilliant ochre sails, barges
with black sails, barges with sails made pale by the powder
of cement, barges with their tackle down ready for towing
up river, barges, in fact, doing everything that a barge can
do. Rochester has been called the City of Barges. I have
endeavoured to present on page 75 a glimpse of this aspect
of things seen as we get out of the Victoria train. It is
reproduced from a water-colour and might well be called a
" bargescape."

The landscape around Rochester is different in type from
that of other parts of the world. The activities of barges
and cement works dominate the scene wherever you may look.
There is a likeness to some of this Rochester riverside landscape

Donald Maxwell

A VIEW FROM ROCHESTER STATION

in the cement re-
gions of the
Thames marshes,
but there the hills
stand so far away
and the completely
" industrialized "
nature of the
country is apt to
be depressing.
There is little to
relieve the indus-
trial monotony.

Rochester : Foreshore and Castle

In Rochester landscape there is another element which harmonizes and tones down the ever-insistent commercial atmosphere. The shipwrights' hammering echoes from the high walls of the Castle. The pinnacles and towers of cement land are not the only pinnacles and towers. The grey Cathedral still rules the sky-line. Walls of mediaeval Rochester still peep out here and there, just to remind us that we should be citizens of no mean city even if many centuries of growth had never been.

As we look down upon the river from the high land of Frindsbury we can read as if written in a book the importance of this crossing of the Medway. There is Rochester Bridge, always a vital link between London and Canterbury, between London and the Continent. Although successive bridges have been built and destroyed, rebuilt and built again, they have all been more or less in the same place, commanded at the southern end by the Castle. The wooded heights visible from here as we look up river are a reminder of the old wooden bridge for the upkeep of which various parishes were responsible, each parish to supply timber and maintain one pier. The name Bridge Woods above Nashenden Valley is a name-relic of those times.

A pageant of the great personages who have crossed the Medway by Rochester Bridge would be a cameo of English history. It may be that Julius Cæsar crossed here ; certainly St. Augustine. The great floods that destroyed London Bridge in 1281 also carried away the wooden bridge at Rochester. It was built up again by 1300 and Edward I crossed on horseback in that year, and the weather was so boisterous that his horse was blown into the river and drowned. Mr. Coles Finch, in his most interesting collection of many years' rambling in and out of Rochester *In Kentish Pilgrim Lands*, records the story, but does not tell us how the king, who was on the horse's back, escaped. Whether or not the king's adventure led to the planning of a better structure is not evident, but it was some forty years later that the bridge was strengthened and rebuilt.

Again an interval of forty years and this stone bridge was commenced, a magnificent structure that lasted till 1856 and is still remembered by many aged inhabitants of Rochester. Over this bridge marched Wat Tyler (1381) and Jack Cade seventy years later. Henry VIII crossed it to behold the much-exaggerated charms of Anne of Cleves, being " marvellously astonished " at her plainness. Charles I and his bride passed this way after their marriage at Canterbury. Charles II rode here in triumph in 1660 on his journey to London at the Restoration, and James II

THE MEDWAY FROM STROOD

crossed it hurriedly and ignominiously in 1688, going the other way.

The strategic importance of Rochester, at this crossing of the river, is obvious, but lest you should miss it you can

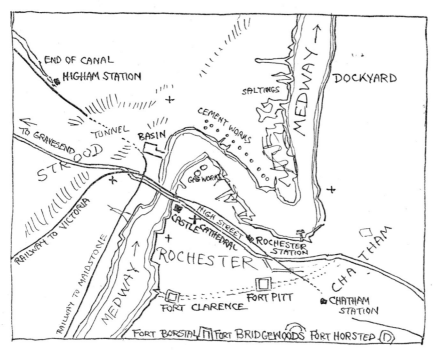

Higham to Chatham

reach it easily, as we have seen from the top of Frindsbury Hill. There is the Castle and the Castle wall and the small zone which represented the defences in the Middle Ages and up to the time of formidable guns. Then if you look farther afield you will see the next chapter in the story—the ring of

forts of earth mounds and brick walls of which Fort Clarence
on the road to Borstal and Fort Pitt visible also above New
Road are easily seen landmarks. Most of these defences
were made at the time of the Napoleonic scare, although
some parts are earlier. Then, as the range of artillery and
its effect become more formidable, these old works have
become obsolete, and you can see another chapter of military
history in the prominent earthworks on the heights farther
out. Fort Borstal, Fort Bridgewoods, and Fort Horsted,
constructed some fifty years ago, are visible from afar. These
were not only the defences of Rochester but the defences of
London against an enemy advancing from the south. All
these are now obsolete, but they still carry on as camping
places from time to time.

The sketch on page 79 is reproduced in monochrome
from a water-colour. I fear it must inevitably lose by the
reduction and by the loss of colour, but it will still show the
unique nature of Medway scenery, with its almost Eastern
effect.

The other two sketches of Rochester on pages 84 and 85
show the narrow street that links Rochester to Chatham.
There is little in it of interest, but a certain dignity is given
to it by the prospect of the Castle, seen to the west in the
left-hand picture. The other sketch is looking the other
way, but taken from the same place in the street. It shows
the quaintness of some of Rochester's wooden buildings.
The surviving examples of this old-time domestic architecture
show many features of interest, especially in canopied door-
ways and carved beam ends, but the encroachment of hideous
modern shop fronts and mean buildings takes away the setting

A NOCTURNE OF ROCHESTER

THE WAY TO CHATHAM

in which they once could give charm and dignity to the street.

The fact that Rochester Bridge is the one and only way of crossing the Medway here is making a difficult problem for those responsible for the organization of road traffic. Another bridge is badly needed. The congestion through Strood is beyond words, very much like Brentford before the new road came. There is nothing, I think, but the cost in the way of sweeping away a good deal of the street to make it wider. With Rochester High Street the problem is different. There are many priceless ancient buildings, which, if they were removed, would destroy Rochester. It is therefore well-nigh impossible to widen the High Street continuously and consistently and in a manner that would make it possible to be a main trunk road.

The trams should never have been allowed to run through this street. The people who were responsible for them coming there thought that they would bring the public in thousands to their shops. But by the subtle irony of time—an irony of which history is full—the trams are now cursed by the same people, for these plebeian obstructions do not allow the wealthy shopper to leave a car at the shop entrance.

A friend of mine the other day suggested a drastic and rather sensational remedy. It is far yet from practical politics, but it has the seeds in it of a possible solution. *Abolish wheeled traffic in the High Street altogether !*

It sounds rather startling at first, but it is only making the High Street akin to Tunbridge Wells in the case of the famous Pantiles. If the wheeled traffic of Rochester were to go some other way it would leave the High Street as a paved Promenade, perhaps planted with trees and boasting outdoor cafés and a good band. Then there would be somewhere to show off fashionable frocks, and Rochester might become another Harrogate or Bath. It is a scheme that has points, even from the shopkeeper's point of view.

The Medway from the Lines, Chatham

DIRGE OF THE WASHINGTON CONFERENCE

THE poet in the days of yore
   Could sing of peace-compelling vows,
Of turning spears to pruning hooks
   And beating sword-blades into ploughs.
But now, when Peace o'erspreads the land
   And War's encrimsoned vision fades,
How shall I sing of giant guns
   Converted into razor-blades ?

I watched a battleship's decease,
   Sad for the havoc peace had wrought.
A Dutchman ruled her iron fate,
   Listing the things contractors bought.
Her guns were gone, her turrets rent ;
   She showed red scars, as streaks of blood,
And like some monster, floating dead,
   Stretched her huge length upon the flood.

O Clio, if on History's page
   The passing of great ships is penned,
Omit all illustration, pray,
   Of such a miserable end ;
Or show her steaming, battle-scarred,
   Straining to challenge desperate odds ;
Or wait till darkness veils the scene
   And show—*the twilight of the gods !*

THE HAUNTED BATTLESHIP

THERE is a small place, rejoicing in the name of Lower Upnor, hard by Chatham, yet separated from it by the River Medway, and difficult of access on account of the large area of the Dockyard, which monopolizes the whole of the opposite shore, with the result that this spot, until recently, has been isolated, and thus retained a rural and primitive character. A castle, from which Queen Elizabeth was wont to review the Fleet, stands at one end, and at the other thick woods climb steeply from the shingle beach, whilst in the middle, where a foreshore, redolent of tar and shavings, discloses picturesque barge-building activities, stands an old-world wooden pier and ruined works with quaint brick towers tucked away under a sky-line of trees.

Relieved against this background of unusual variety appears the great mass of the much-depleted battleship *Conqueror* in the hands of the shipbreakers. Her funnels, masts, and superstructure have gone. Only her turrets remain. Her long 13·5 inch guns are " sawn off " to stumpy

The " Conqueror " in the hands
of the ship-breakers, Upnor

*" The deck was strewn with steel plates cut up into
fragments, with gratings, heaps of bolts, pieces of
funnel casing, and other ship-breakers' litter "*

caricatures of trench mortars, and there is little to proclaim
her vanished power but her challenging bow and her giant
length as she stretches, like Ophiuchus huge, upon the waters.
Floating cranes are at work, and busy shifts of men removing
great pieces of metal to be sold.

It is in some ways a sad sight to a Naval man, who
remembers her as a crack ship, the latest of the super-
Dreadnoughts just twelve years ago, and it is not a very

thrilling one to anybody. There is a certain pathos about this giant being ruthlessly pulled to pieces for the value of her metal. How are the mighty fallen, not through failure but through success? How much a ton will the commercial world give for old steel? The weapons of war, how are they perished? There may, however, be poetic justice in seeing a German submarine share this fate, as the one which is lying at Chatham like a huge black monster of the deep will undoubtedly do.

My ghost story begins in broad daylight—to be exact, at high noon; for it was when the men were just knocking off for their dinner that I rowed alongside and mounted a perilous gangway to gain the quarter-deck. I was met by a scene of utter desolation and by a Dutchman—some of the Dutch are still in the Medway—who was in charge of the shipbreaking work, and who courteously explained many things in the shipbreaking line which I should have been unable to fathom by myself. Then he left me to wander about alone.

The deck was strewn with steel plates cut up into fragments, with gratings, heaps of bolts, pieces of funnel-casing, and other shipbreakers' litter.

I found my way into the ruined wardroom (the black cavity of which can be seen on the right-hand side of the sketch on page 93), and sat down upon a broken box, the only hospitality it offered. The wardroom of the *Conqueror* is, or was, in the fore part of the ship. Vistas of woodland landscape appeared through rents in the steel walls, an eerie compensation for the absence of pictorial decoration. Through a gaping hole, where the piano had

GHOSTS

stood, I could discern two lugubrious-looking workmen cooking steak and onions. The cheery genius of the ward-room was dead, and this burnt sacrifice of steak and onions made nightmare incense at its solemn obsequies. The walls, dirty, rusted, or burnt by the ever-consuming attack of the blow-flame, seemed to close me in ominously, and I felt as though I were seated within a huge and empty skull. The atmosphere, without prejudice to the onions, was depressing, for here had been the focus of the camaraderie of the ship and a place of infinite jest. I was moved to mutter, " Where be your gibes now ? your gambols ? and your songs ? your flashes of merriment, that were wont to set the table in a roar ? "

Then a strange thing happened. Dim forms took shape, and I could see the Commander balancing a glass of port as he talked with " Guns," the Doctor and the Pay arguing, and the Chief tossing for drinks with a shadowy form.

Besides all that, strange voices rose and fell, a pianola made mad mechanical music, and all the world went merrily as though a rumour had been discovered of the German Fleet coming out. And, stranger still, these were not ghosts of dead heroes, or of the old-time *Conqueror's* wardroom of the past, but of living men. Strangest of all, some of them must have been at that moment in the smoking-room of the Naval Barracks not two miles away. I will give no explanation, but merely record what I saw.

Then the room thinned. *Conqueror* is in action. It is Jutland. The Day has come ! Deafening broadsides, and smoke and fire, and I had awoke from my reverie to find myself in perilous proximity to a flame attack on the

F

fifteen-inch armour of the conning tower. I left hurriedly, and let the Upnor Shipbreaking Company get on with razor-blades and mowing-machines to enrich life in these times of peace.

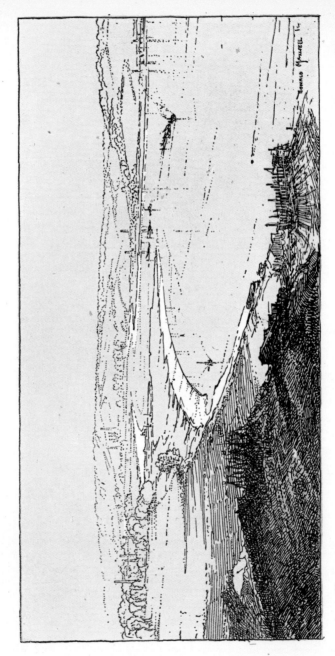

VI
Pilgrims and Strangers

MEDWAY HEIGHTS

THERE is magic in the Medway,
  There's a spell upon the tide.
  —O here, up here, is the place to be.
There's a glamour and a glitter
Where misty barges glide.
    —O here, up here, is the place for me.
From Rochester to Maidstone
  A golden glory thrills.
We have found the lost Atlantis
  In the hollow of the hills.

There is magic in the morning,
There's a tang about the air.
    —O here, up here, is the place to be.
The sun's right up,
But the world's not there!
    —O here, up here, is the place for me.
We look upon a billowy lake
  Of vapours, white as snow,
And gold-topped chimneys sticking up
  From the busy world below.

There is magic in the noonday
And the tide is at the flood.
    —O here, up here, is the place to be.
Cement is turned to ivory:
There's gold instead of mud.
    —O here, up here, is the place for me.
I saw the marsh become a land
  Where crystal rivers flowed;
And I've seen the Walls of Sion
  From the top of Borstal Road.

A pilgrims' road

PILGRIMS AND STRANGERS

THE Pilgrims' Road from London to Canterbury, the road of which Chaucer writes, coincides with the Watling Street of the Romans and passes through Rochester. The Pilgrims' Way from Winchester to Canterbury keeps to the south side of the chalk ridge of the North Downs.   The point at which this course crossed the Medway is generally judged to have been from Upper Halling, through Snodland, to Burham and Boxley, leaving the chalk ridge for the marsh and picking it up again on the other side of the river.

The Medway here has carved a way towards the north, and the sides of the valley are as a V with Rochester at the angle.   There must have been times, however, when the river was in flood, or for other reasons, when the pilgrims would have continued along the track to Strood, crossed Rochester Bridge and struck out again—after a pious pause to behold the wonders of Rochester Cathedral and perhaps taste of the good red wine made by the monks. They would then take the track by the river, now Borstal Road, and thus join the Pilgrims' Way again above Burham.

This track from Rochester is marked by the Ordnance Survey as a Pilgrim road, and from the top of the hill, as the traveller leaves Borstal on the Wouldham Road, he will see it without doubt. I have sketched it at the head of this chapter as it appears from across a field in which the Ordnance map marks a dotted line, cutting off the corner between the Wouldham road and the road to Burham.

This way, as it winds over the shoulder of the hill, *looks* like a Pilgrims' road and whenever I see it, as I so often do, I feel a sense of adventure, for here is a type of life's road seen only for a little way ahead, yet full of hopes and

A glimpse of Wouldham

The road to Burham

possibilities and holding fair promise of a glorious vista on the other side of the hill.

I had started out one morning upon the road to Boxley Abbey, which lies farther on and on the Pilgrims' Way proper, and I had reached the foot of the hill (seen on page 103) when I chanced to overtake two pedestrians. They were men, armed as I was, with painting gear, apparently artists and apparently, also, so strong was the likeness between them, father and son.

I fell in with them and we walked together, discoursing on landscape and exploring in general. The older of the two seemed at home in the Medway valley, and evidently knew it well as a sketching ground. To the younger, however, it was evidently new.

"I find it most exciting," he said. "The whole region is packed full of history and quaint domestic architecture—but we ought to have come for our tour before there were any cement works."

Lunar landscape at Wouldham

"On the other hand," the elder one put in, "I *like* the cement works—that is, where there are plenty of them."

"There are plenty of them here in all conscience," retorted

the younger; "the more there are, the worse becomes the scenery."

I tried to hold the balance between these rival schools of taste and held that cement works were like a certain little girl who, when she was nice was very nice, indeed, but

A cottage by the way: Burham

when she was bad was horrid. It is the transition stage that is so painful, when the country is being spoilt and the town has not begun.

"Yes," argued the younger, "God made the country; man made the town."

"I do not agree with you at all," the elder man protested. "That is a saying often quoted quite inaptly. If by country you mean primeval forests, and the trackless wastes of the everlasting hills, I might possibly agree with you. But you don't mean that. You mean in effect that God made that ploughed field, those haystacks and this hedge, whereas man (or the Amalgamated Portland Cement Manufacturers) made the cement works, and those chimneys. All these things are the

An ecclesiastical barn: Boxley Abbey

A box tree at Boxley

works of man and not of nature. One not more so than the other."

" Hold ! One is more of nature than the other," protested the younger. " The countryman is nature's assistant. He ploughs and sows and reaps, but it is the forces of nature at work that are the charm and romance of the country."

" Not so," the elder continued. " When I was your age, I thought as you did, but now that I am older I see more and more the romance of man's labour. Man is like an insect upon the earth, tiny and weak and at times almost appalled

Old houses at Bearsted

Leeds Castle

by the crushing vastness of the forces against him. But for all that he is only a little lower than the angels, and he is born to conquer his environment. Millions of years ago this chalk land was ooze at the bottom of the sea. The mud in the river-bed is the silt of lost continents. The carbon which is pouring from those chimneys is the improperly consumed remnants of a forest of giant ferns. These are being rearranged to make dwelling places in cities—and then men say there is no romance in the housing problem!"

By this time we had arrived at a point above Wouldham, and I pointed out to these visitors that the strange place upon which we looked down, similar to what I should imagine is the sort of landscape to be seen on the moon, was a quarry which had helped to make history. A part of it is known as Zeebrugge, and the local tradition, and one that can be borne out with ample evidence, is to the effect that here some of the men were trained for the great Naval raid. Scaling practice and all manner of climbing could be indulged in here to the heart's intent. At the time, I remember, it was rumoured that these strenuous drills were for the purpose of landing in Heligoland.

I parted with my artist friends at Burham, they going on to Aylesford, while I kept to the upper road, which is now the proper and authentic Pilgrims' Way. Boxley Abbey lies to the right of the Way. There is not much to see but the huge barn, but that alone is worth many days' travel. I have scribbled down a small note of the lower part of the building. It is a barn every turn of which reminds you of a church.

Although there is now little remaining at Boxley to tell of its one-time great importance as a Cistercian monastery it has played no small part in the history of England, for it was here that Cardinal Campeggio (from Rome) and Archbishop Warham held counsel and decreed against the divorce of Henry VIII. This decree, backed by full Papal authority, caused the King to look for spiritual supporters who were all ready to break with the Papacy. Thus the King got Anne Boleyn and the country got the glorious Reformation, but after some four hundred years many good people have their doubts as to whether it was all quite so glorious as it promised to be.

For an interesting and not too technical account of Boxley

DONALD MAXWELL

LEEDS CASTLE : THE MOAT

Abbey, I recommend you to read Mr. Coles Finch's notes in his book, *In Kentish Pilgrim Lands*. Incidentally we learn that the name Boxley is not derived (as some have asserted) from the fact that the hill-clad slopes near abounded with box trees. It is to the beech tree that Boxley owes its name, " which is in effect the ' beech-tree lea ' or the place of ' bocs ' or beeches."

Soon the Way becomes a grass track and there are woods climbing the ridge to the left, and green glades cut into them like glaciers of grass coming down from the heights. After another mile or so I determined to strike out at right-angles and make for the Weald, which lies beyond the ragstone hills. This brought me to Bearsted, the last houses of which (I mean last in order of travel) I have sketched on page 108. They are typical timbered buildings of the old Kentish style.

Then I came to Leeds Castle, perhaps the most perfect and least modernized example of a feudal castle in the South of England. The first view that the traveller sees is that from the road above the Park Gate Inn, and I have sketched this on page 109, but by taking a footpath across the park (there is a right of way through it) many other wonderful prospects are disclosed. The castle in its present form was rebuilt by William of Wykeham about 1350, and it stands on three islands in a small lake formed by the little River Len.

The curfew bell can still be heard in England, and this is one of the places where it is rung. Henry VIII was in the habit of coming here, but without a book of reference I dare not hazard a guess as to which of his wives was the attraction on the occasions of his visits. Previously Edward I had been another royal resident at Leeds, and the traditional

G

story about the Boathouse is that it was built as a swimming bath for that monarch.

I made a sketch of the moat before I left (page 112), and a thumb-nail note of the very massive and square tower of Leeds Church (page 136), and then sought the Weald. By some good fortune, however, I wandered on and came to it not by the shortest route, but by one most circuitous, and one that led through the Valley of Dreams.

So unexpected is this valley that the traveller may miss it altogether. It is so beautiful that he will imagine he is walking in a trance and expect any minute to be awakened.

Woodlands above Boxley

VII

The Valley of Dreams

A RIDDLE OF KENT

I KNOW of a valley enchanted,
   A valley of crystalline streams,
A valley of Kent in a mountain,
   —I call it the Valley of Dreams.

I sing of an emerald Eden,
   Gold-barred by the morning's beams,
But I tell you nought of the road I sought
   To come to the Valley of Dreams.

I fear the men of the moment,
   I fear their hurrying schemes,
I fear the rush of the motor,
   Destroying my Valley of Dreams.

So I give you the clue of the waters,
   To follow the light that gleams.
Who readeth the riddle of Langley,
   Discovers the Valley of Dreams.

THE VALLEY OF DREAMS

I HAVE called it the Valley of Dreams, for it stands apart from this work-a-day world. It is a valley where time stands still, where geography gets lost, where geology is suspended, and where even the laws of gravitation are slightly modified.

As a rest from the general rush and hurry of modern life I know no better antidote and no surer sedative than a walk through its woodland ways or a pause by its crystal streams. I do not speculate as to whether or not inanimate things can dream as we do, but if ever any landscape can dream, it is the landscape of this valley.

The slopes that rise from its waters dream that Kent is

in the Himalayas, and therefore they are a fitting part of the mountain scenery. The old timbered houses that stand at one end of this hollow dream that good Queen Bess is still on visiting terms with the Weald and so give her a welcome by looking as prosperous and comfortable as possible. The mill-ponds, of which there are five within a short distance, are dreaming, dreaming of the mills that have gone. Even the trees are dreaming, dreaming that they are dancing down the valley, drawn by the sweet melody of Orpheus. They seem to bend and swing and sway in ordered pause, as if they had stopped for a moment and were just waiting to go on again.

I do not tell you the whereabouts of the Valley of Dreams,

" The old timbered houses that stand at one end of this hollow dream that good Queen Bess is still on visiting terms with the Weald "

" Even the trees are dreaming, dreaming that they are dancing down the valley, drawn by the sweet melody of Orpheus "

not because I am selfish or misanthropic, but because I fear to write down in a book, for all men to see, the position of this haunt, lest it may be opened to the prying of the vulgar and the attention of the rich. I will, therefore, throw a disguise about the geography of the place that I may succeed in preventing multitudes of people from thronging thither in cars and thus causing its seclusion to vanish away. The good people who have sought this valley and found it, and the good people who live in it, these will smile at my cunning—

and bless me. The many who know it well and delight in
it will welcome as friends those others of good intent who
can find it—and you, dear reader, are assuredly of the number.
By means of clues let drop in these pages those kindred spirits
who can read between the lines will get there. The saints
be praised : the roads are very bad !

The names I have chosen here and set down upon the
little map of clues on page 126 are some of them evolved out
of my own fancy, and some are names in use to-day among
the people of the Valley of Dreams. Within a small area—
a surprisingly small area—are many types and beauties of
famous places far away, places whither people will travel at
great pains. If the fame of this haunt does not compare
with their fame, its beauties compare bravely with their
beauties.

I do not say that the spacious wooden houses of the
Odenwald are not more numerous than the old wooden houses
here, but they are not more pleasing to look at. I do not
say that the green declivities of Alpine pastures are not
situated at a higher sea-level than these green declivities, but
they are not more picturesque.

I do not say that the Pools of Solomon are not larger in
area than the pools in this valley, but they are not more
delectable on a summer morning. I do not say that the
heart of the Black Forest is not farther from London than
this spot, but it is not more silent or more still upon a starlit
night.

The first clue to this mysterious spot is the clue of the
steps to the spring. I have sketched the place you must
find at the very beginning of things. If you are in a car

" A TYPE OF ARCHITECTURE THAT
IS GENEROUS IN SCALE AND
SATISFYING IN PROPORTION "

you must keep a sharp look-out, for you may pass over this arch in the stonework (see sketch on page 127), but you will see the little round basin and the conduit leading down the valley. It runs at first through gardens and is joined by similar little stone-edged conduits. There is something about these waterways through the vegetable world that reminds me of the Lebanon Mountains. I remember walking for ten miles or so from Beirut, more or less on the Damascus road, and I came to many gardens embanked and terraced on the hills. Somehow or other these irrigated gardens remind me of those places.

As in the East, where fountains and wells like this are associated with water-carriers, so, for all the progress of rural district councils, this eastern-looking garden realm is a place for the carrying of water to the houses above. The arch in the sketch passes under the road and leads from a row of stone cottages. Upon these is an engraved stone, bearing a highly commendable, but rather quaintly expressed, sentiment, and showing that just a hundred years has elapsed since it was put up.

I have twice been to this place to write down the inscription and I have twice lost what I have written down and so, now that I come to this last proof, with a gap still in it, I must quote from memory. It is to the effect that with sobriety, contentment, industry and cleanliness a poor man may live " happy and content." The stone is dated 1827. It was from a raised plot of garden across the road from this row of cottages that I made the sketch reproduced on page 118.

There are some old stone buildings, malthouses, at this

end of the valley, disclosing a type of architecture that is generous in scale and satisfying in proportion. The half-timbered cottages beyond them were here before Queen Elizabeth came to the throne, and they are well worth a long pilgrimage to see.

The extraordinary steepness of the hillsides below this point are to be accounted for by no geological formation

" I do not say that the Pools of Solomon are not larger in area than the pools in this valley, but they are not more delectable upon a summer morning "

" The slopes that rise from its waters dream that Kent is in the Himalayas "

known to Kent, and are the result of quarries having been worked here, but at some far distant date. Some say that the Romans worked this place and that it is possible that some of the stones in the Roman wall of London were hewn out of these valley sides. Others say that at the time of the Conquest large demands were made on this stone for church building, and that this demand continued and increased through the Middle Ages until the valley was fashioned in the form in which we see it to-day.

It is known, too, that cannon balls were made out of this hard rag-stone in the early days of cannon, when iron was too costly and too rare to be used in large quantities. No

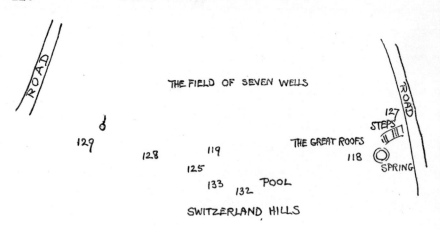

A clue-map to the Valley of Dreams

doubt the stone, breaking into fragments when the projectile hit a fortress, would act as a kind of shrapnel.

At a certain point below the hill-top, shown on page 125, there is a division in the path, which has become narrow, stony and steep, and in wet weather very muddy. The path to the right dips down and then crosses the valley, ascending on the northern side. The other path, however, ascends and becomes a narrow track, hanging upon the wooded side of the ridge.

At this point I paused to gaze upon the scene (as portrayed on page 128), wondering whether or no this pool of water, so like an artificial lake, had ever been a mill-pond. As I stood there I was joined by the genius of the valley—or if he was not the genius he looked as if he might be. He was an old man and he told me many things about this place, close to which he had been born, and in which he had lived nearly all his life.

The point that impressed him most was the fact that I was making inquiries about the history of the place, and had nothing with me but a small book. Hitherto, his experience of historians, antiquaries, and other eccentric people, had been that they all had large books of reference—the more learned the man the larger the book.

" It was just at the back o' this hill," he said, " that Bill and me—that is Bill Somers, not George, who went to America —found some coins, all rusty, and dirty, but wonderful old-fashioned. I showed 'em to a man what was a sort o' local preacher in the Salvation Army, and he says as 'ow they might be valuable, and he writes to the British Museum, tellin' 'em about it and 'ow Bill and me would be quite willin' to sell any o' these old things reasonable or exchange 'em for ordinary money what we could spend.

" The next day," he continued, " down comes a scholard with a book and 'e gets quite excited and tells us he will pay us well if we leaves off and goes to the ' Green Dragon ' while he gets all the professors down from London.

" ' It's helpin' the cause o' Hinglish 'istory,' he says.

" Well, arter that I says to

The clue of the steps to the spring

" The mill-ponds, of which there are five within a short distance, are dreaming . . ."

Bill, ' Lord forbid the likes of us should put hany hobstacle in the way of Hinglish 'istory,' so off we goes to the ' Green Dragon,' and we stops there sort o' contented like.

" Next mornin' two more scholards come and one of 'em had a book as big as a church bible. Pickshers in it, too. And bless me if 'e didn't show me the coins wot Bill and me 'ad found—all drord in the book as nat'ral as a photigraph. Well, all that day we digged for 'em—except when we was

a-makin' Hinglish 'istory in the ' Green Dragon '—and we
found all sorts o' things.

"Next day arter that another of 'em come over and 'e
'ad a book larger 'an any of 'em, and 'e comes up and shakes
'ands with Bill and me as if we was dooks and said as 'ow we
had done a great service to the cause of astronomy, and he
gives us a golden sov'reign apiece and tells us he will be only
too pleased to pay us for anything else we finds."

" And did you ever make further discoveries ? " I asked,
now quite roused into interest by his graphic description.

" .   . dreaming of the mills that have gone ,,

H

" N'er a one," he replied sadly. " All we ever found arter that was a large kettle with the spout broke. It wasn't no good tryin' to pass it off as belongin' to the Ancient Britons 'cos they always made kettles out o' flints, so parson told us."

We talked for a while and he told me more of the doings of himself and his mate, but they were rather of a personal than antiquarian interest. I asked him if the lagoon at our feet had ever been a mill-pond.

" I can't say," he replied, " but once, when Bill and me was workin' at the Manshun we 'ad a job to empty out the water and clear it all out. Then we finds something funny, but I don't think it 'ad anything to do with astronomy."

I think my friend meant archæology, but I did not like to stop the flow of his narrative.

" What we finds," he continued, " was a lot of cows' 'orns. There were too many for it to be cows what had been drinkin' and fell in—I did hear as 'ow there was once a tannery here and it may be there was a mill as well—before my time, though."

He told me that the field below us and across the stream that flowed out of this circular pond was known as Seven-Wells Field on account of the fact that seven separate springs arise within it. He also told me that the ridges on this side of the valley (where they overhang the pool, shown on pages 132 and 133) are known as Switzerland Hills. I have indicated their position on the clue map on page 126. And then we parted ; he taking the lower path across the valley, and I continuing towards the west.

" I DO NOT SAY THAT THE HEART OF THE BLACK FOREST IS NOT FARTHER FROM LONDON
THAN THIS SPOT, BUT IT IS NOT MORE SILENT ON A STARLIT NIGHT "

"I DO NOT SAY THAT THE SPACIOUS TIMBERED HOUSES OF THE ODENWALD ARE NOT MORE NUMEROUS THAN THE TIMBERED HOUSES HERE, BUT THEY ARE NOT MORE ROMANTIC IN THEIR GREEN SETTING"

" Thank you, sir. To the cause of Hinglish 'istory—and your very good 'ealth, too, sir."

The woodland path comes out by a pond, the water from which is working a ram to supply a house on the hill with water. This ram is upon the site of an old mill, the last of the mills to disappear from this valley. It has gone quite recently, and now where there were five there is not even one.

At the lower end of the valley are many houses, and soon the explorer comes to a village with quaint riverside cottages, each with a little bridge across the stream. There are little brooks gushing out of the hillside and hurrying merrily to join the main stream. At one point a rivulet of water accompanies the road. The noise of waters and the stony banks, moss-grown here and there, remind me both of the Lake district and of the Black Forest. Yet the whole of this delightful valley is so near to a town. It seems impossible.

Below the village the valley turns and again there is silence under the hill. I have stood here by starlight, with just a light or two of the last cottages still showing at the bend. It is indeed a Valley of Dreams, for it is easy to dream here that you are far from towns (although you are quite near one) and far from railways (although you are not two miles away from one).

I hope that the curious situation of this valley will protect it from being exploited. That is why I have hesitated to put down in black and white exactly where it is. You will long ago have read the riddle, even if you did not know it when you started on the chapter. But hundreds and hundreds from London and afar will have to seek a little before they find, and thus too many will not arrive at once and crowd out romance. Long may this happy valley remain the Valley of Dreams.

Leeds Church.

VIII

The Vineyards of the North

THE CASTLES OF KENT

O PEOPLE they come from far and wide
With a Morris car and a shilling guide ;
And a man may reckon his time well spent
Counting the castle walls of Kent.
Dover, Rochester, so he reads,
Tonbridge, Allington, Upnor, Leeds—
These are the scenes of doughty deeds.

And when he is looking around for these
He notices, hidden among the trees,
Curious towers with conical tops
—They're hundreds strong in the land of hops—
" *What are they ?* "   Surely a child can tell.
" *These are the castles of Kent as well.*"

Freedom ! the man of Kent's one boast.
For freedom stands the friendly oast,
Guarding our land from killjoy raiders
And prohibitionist invaders.
Long may the Kentish hop-fields thrive !
Long may the castles of Kent survive !

CASTLES OF KENT

THE VINEYARDS OF THE NORTH

I WALKED on and on. The stars were out. The dim and mysterious light they gave turned dense darkness into a luminous darkness so that it was possible to *feel* where things were even if it was impossible to *see* them. I did not know in the least where I had come to. Leaving the valley behind, I had climbed to a level plateau and walked by means of footpaths through nut plantations. For a mile or so I seemed to be on high land, and then my path, still a mere track through the fields, became a steep descent.

My direction, as I could see from the stars, was almost due south, so that I judged that I had come to the " floor " of the Weald. I came to a road and still continued, but like so many of these old roads in the country it progressed by a series of right-angle turns which take the traveller in almost every direction from time to time. There was still a bias, however, one way, and such succession of bearings as west, north-west, south-west, south-east, north-east, south-east, south, south-west, etc., still tended to advance my march in a southerly direction.

On this night, a night early in September, there seemed to be such a quality of freshness in the air that it was exhilarating to walk on without aim or object. I could not tell you wherein this fascination lay, for it was impossible to see anything: yet undoubtedly there was a " call " in the night.

One of the effects of this walking through the night when nothing is visible is an increased sense of level. It is possible to notice ups and downs of a few feet only which in daylight would probably not be apparent. The " floor " of the Weald always seems curious to me from the fact that it is nearly a level plain but not quite level. Marshland has its occasional bumps and mounds, but this level of the Weald rises and falls (from the surrounding levels) over large areas by a few feet—ten feet, twenty feet, occasionally fifty feet, but not more.

My wanderings in the Weald had now covered so many hours that the next event would be the dawn. By this time I had turned and was making some way towards the north-west. I was now on ascending ground again and must have been, as far as I could judge, about a hundred feet high, and somewhere in the neighbourhood of East Farleigh.

A faint green-grey showed in the east and I could make

THE HOPPERS' SATURDAY NIGHT

out the hop-poles and other features of this côte-d'or of our northern vineyards. Being the first week in September, the land was full of nomadic Londoners, and the smoke from countless fires bore witness to the annual invasion. Some of the hop-pickers were already astir and as soon as it was light there were groups of them standing round the fires and making preparations for breakfast.

In spite of the fact that I had been walking vigorously for hours, I was not any too warm, for the morning breeze was cold, and I came near to one of these cheery blazes, the good-natured Londoners giving me a hospitable welcome.

"Come along, sir, and make yourself at home." I thanked them and found a seat upon an overturned basket. One of the men who had looked at me fixedly as I warmed myself came up and said, "Blowed if I didn't think you was a ghost, Mr. Maxwell! It ain't the first time I've made up a fire for you at the *Graphic*, is it, sir?"

It was old Bob, night-watchman at Tallis Street in the days of the war. This incident of meeting of Fleet Street comrades gave me a higher status than ever with the hop-pickers, and I was invited to breakfast forthwith.

"You ain't altered a bit, sir," said Bob. "When I sees yer comin' along with your big sketch book, I ses to meself, I ses, 'There's that there naval horficer what I used to look after—dressed as a gentleman.'"

This was an allusion to my naval days (before I was an official artist to the Admiralty) when, with a few hours' leave, I used to turn up at the *Graphic*, sometimes by night, and (with Admiralty permission and censorship) execute a drawing of some incident of life on the fringes of the Fleet. On these occasions the faithful Bob would stoke up an immense fire, bring me huge rations of tea and buns, and produce blankets for me to sleep in for the few hours I might steal out of the night's work.

These blankets (a strange product, it would seem, for a newspaper office if their nature was not known) were printing blankets, used for clothing the cylinder on which the sheets of the *Daily Graphic* were run in a rotary machine. As warmth they were effective, but the fact that images of the last few days' photographs registered upon them invariably came off on my face and hands, transforming me temporarily into a pictorial news-sheet, had its disadvantages. There was a danger, too, that on my return to duties upon the North Sea, I might fall into the hands of some hostile sub-marine, and, with these designs upon me, convey information to the enemy.

It is a fortunate thing for me our law-makers in framing the special regulations for the defence of the realm, knew nothing about these "living pictures." Otherwise, judging from the fact that many grotesque war-time restrictions are still in force, I should probably be forbidden to have blankets on my bed at all. Our intelligent legislators would no doubt keep the regulation in force for another ten years or so, and life would be exceedingly uncomfortable.

We talked of these nights in "The Street of Adventure." "Don't you remember, sir, when I had to be a model for you—a sailor with a hovercoat and 'ood (what made me look like a monk) and with your walkin'-stick to represent a machine-gun? Lor', sir, I didn't 'alf get chaffed about that.

IN THE GARDEN OF ENGLAND

It went all round as 'ow I'd been a model, and the machine men used to shout out : ' Look out, Bill, 'ere comes Hepstein's Wenus.' "

I found, after further conversation with these visitors, that the general exodus from London in September is nothing like what it was. Owing to the raised standard of camping accommodation for the hoppers, the farmers are unable to employ so many pickers from a distance. They depend more and more on local daily labour from Maidstone and surrounding places. Motor transport enables them to get to the hop-fields from some distance and return again at night.

The scenes in these " vineyards of the north "—although there is present an element of squalor—are often exceedingly " picturesque," and the scenes at the time of picking are comparable with the scenes in the wine countries of Southern Europe. I have sketched here two aspects of these gardens —one on page 141, where the oast-houses, ever-present in the sky-line, appear as towers in a château country, and one at evening, which I have called " A Hopper's Saturday Night." Enterprising tradesmen from Maidstone hold a kind of fair at various points at this season for the sale of provisions and even clothing. Nor is the Church less adaptable, for there are tents, writing-rooms, and nightly concerts or recreations. There is a nurse with ambulance appliances, a very valuable help, for many minor accidents, and not a few serious ones, occur from time to time during the picking.

Some of the earliest varieties of hops are picked in the last week of August, and the latest are not always cleared until well into October. The hops when gathered are cured by means of a sulphur smoke in the oast-houses, and they come out a rich brown colour. These oast-houses are so much a feature of Kentish scenery that it is impossible to contemplate prohibition for artistic reasons alone—to say nothing of its inherent stupidity.

Chateau d'Oast

IX

The Lost Waters of Langley

THE LOYALTY OF THE WEALD

THEY say as how in Switzerland,
　　Where all the grand folk go,
There's mountains—in the summer-time—
　　With tops all white wi' snow.
I ain't got nothin' agin them parts,
　　But I tell you fair and square
I don't suppose they're half as grand
　　As Boughton Hill up there.
Yes, Boughton Hill in spring, my lad,
　　With trees all gay and green,
An' white clouds peeping over th' top
　　—As pretty as ever *I've* seen.

They say as how in France and Spain
　　They cultivate the vine,
And you see the folk in fancy dress
　　A-dancin' and makin' wine.
I ain't got nothin' agin them parts,
　　But I tell you, fair and square,
I don't suppose they've ever seen
　　A field of hops out there !
Yes, a field of Kentish hops, my lad,
　　All climbing up in rows
To make good cheer wi' Kentish beer
　　—As good as ever *I* knows.

They say as how in Italy
　　There's palaces in ruins
And scholards writin' history books
　　On Julius Cæsar's doin's.
I ain't got nothin' agin them parts,
　　But I tell you, fair and square,
Old Julius Cæsar come to Kent !
　　—Just for to get the air.
So there ain't no need for gadding about,
　　Whatever you be at.
You'll be content in the Weald o' Kent :
　　—*And I can't say fairer 'an that !*

Brishing Farm

THE LOST WATERS OF LANGLEY

THE tactics I employed in continuing my ramble after leaving the hop gardens of East Farleigh were very similar to those employed by the good old Duke of York on the historic occasion when he marched a large force (I cannot remember the exact number) to the top of the hill and marched them down again. Future historians, however, will no doubt notice two important variations. Although history repeated itself, the repetition was not mechanically the same. In the first place, there were not so many of us employed in this subtle manœuvre. I was alone. In the second place, I marched *from* the top of the hill and then marched *up* again,

*East Hall Farm : Gateway surmounted
by Cottage Loaf*

thus inventing a strikingly original plan of campaign which will no doubt be studied carefully by military tacticians.

I had kept along the rag-stone ridge in an easterly direction until I had come to a point near Boughton Monchelsea where there is a farm, not unlike a French château (page 151). Some of the farm buildings are fashioned out of the base of oast-houses and thus have a castle-like appearance. Then I continued to the edge of the ridge, where it dips down suddenly to the south, overlooking the broad levels of the Weald, and came to East Hall Farm with its cluster of oast-houses.

The gate into the farm-house garden is a fine piece of stonework and possesses a curious feature. The summit of the gable is surmounted by a cottage loaf in stone. Its significance is doubtful. Was it once the bakery of the estate or a sign of the hospitality of a guest house, or has it possibly come from some earlier monastic work now replaced.

I found nobody about and so could not make any inquiries, but descended the steep hill and wandered in the level country at its feet.

Here I made a sketch (page 155) showing one of the

numerous half-timbered houses that are scattered so thickly through this part. As I was completing the sketch a fellow traveller came up and we exchanged intelligence as to the land we were in. He told me of wonders of which I had never read—of the Lost Water of Langley, a freak of geology mentioned by Lambarde in his *Perambulation of Kent*.

This intelligence immediately altered my plans, and that is why I marched up the hill again. At East Hall Farm I

East Hall Farm

was fortunate enough to run to earth a source of information, and in the library of Rock House, Boughton Monchelsea, I was able to study, by the kind invitation of the Hon. Henry Hannen, the owner, a contemporary manuscript copy of Lambarde's great work. I also looked up other references.

Hasted (1790) writes : " The stream which runs at Langley about a mile from thence at Brishling loses itself underground, running through a subterraneous passage for near half a mile, from which circumstance this parish is supposed to take its name" (Loose). Camden does not refer to this underground river, or I was unsuccessful in finding a reference. His tribute to Lambarde, however, and his indebtedness to him is worth quoting for its quaintness:

" Now am I come to Kent, which Countrey although master William Lambard, a man right well endued with excellent learning, and as godly vertues, hath so lively depainted out in a full volume, that his painefull felicitie in that kind hath left little, or nothing for others, yet according to the project of this worke which I have taken in hand, I will runne it over also ; and least any man should thinke, that as the Comicall Poet saith, *I deale by way of close pilfering* I willingly acknowledge him (and desire he doth no lesse) to have beene my foundation, and fountaine both of all (well neere) that I shall say."

Here is the reference from Lambarde's work, *A Perambulation of Kent, conteining the description, historie and customes of that shire*, published just 400 years ago (1576):

" There ariseth, neare to the Parke and Hothe of Langley, a small spring, which at Brishyng (about one mile off) falleth into the ground, and hideth itselfe, being conveighed under the earth neare to Cockshothe, by the space of half a mile, and then at a great Pitte of the Quarrey, discovereth it selfe againe, and runneth above grounde to Loose (I wot not, whether so called of this Losse) between which place, and the mouth thereof (which powreth into Medway at Tovelle,

A Cottage in the Weald

betweene Maidstone and Eastfarley, and exceedeth not two miles in lengthe) it beareth thirteen Fulling Milles and one for Corne, which are reputed to earne so many hundreds of pounds by the yeere. This thing I was rather occasioned to note, by viewing the course of the water in that Mappe, where you may see it broken off, as if it were crossed with a bridge of land, and that purposely, to shew the secretes of this Chanell."

I have always held that for information on topographical subjects the last people to consult are the inhabitants of a village. They hardly ever know anything about the place.

By Langley Church : the source of the stream

Some of the dwellers in Langley are no exception to the general rule.

Upon a Sunday afternoon, at a corner not far from the church, I interrogated a group of ten or a dozen youths on the subject, herebefore mentioned, of the stream that loses itself and appears again.

None of them had heard of it and all vehemently denied that there was any stream in Langley at all—or anywhere

The Lake of Langley

near it. Had I not been so well used to astonishing local ignorance I should have gone away, without further search, under this impression that Lambarde and Hasted must have referred to some other place named Langley.

K

However, I persisted in my quest and found a stream within 200 yards of the place where they were standing. I have sketched the springhead, its origin, in the heading to this chapter.

After a few hundred yards, this brook enters Langley Park and broadens out into a small lake about one-third of a mile long and, at the broader and lower end, some 200 feet wide.

At the western extremity and on the left bank is a house known as Langley Ponds (sketched on page 159). This name recalls the chain of trout ponds formerly covering the area now occupied by the lake.

A small cottage or hop-picker's shelter has been converted into a boat-house in the middle of the lake. Hop gardens come down to the water on one side and a nut plantation on the other. Many trees have been planted along the waterside walk on the northern shore and, delightful as it is, this lake promises to be still more delightful in the years to come.

Below this spot the brook runs merrily along through an osier bed and alongside a field of hops till it comes out into an open and marshy grassland. There is a little brick bridge, evidently for sheep and cattle, for nothing but turf rests upon it. Beyond this a by-road crosses the stream and we come to another osier bed. Then we find a footpath on its right bank and we discover mysterious little sluices and something that makes a noise underground and a trap-door. No doubt this is a ram for pumping water up to Brishing Farm, which we begin to see on the left upon rising ground.

Then we come to another by-road and just beyond it a

LANGLEY PONDS

small sluice and what is evidently a sheep-wash. After this point the formation of the land is very curious. The stream runs along the right-hand side of a broad trench, which may once have been excavated for its stone. Can it be that at one time, possibly a thousand years ago, this stream was

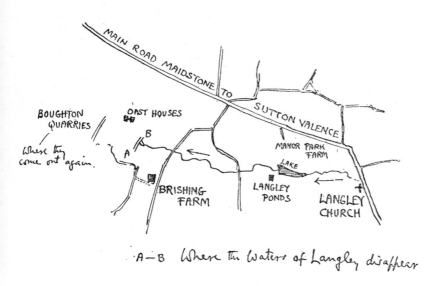

A—B Where the Waters of Langley disappear

much bigger and that a flaw in the bed on which it flows has let the water run away?

The vanishing of this stream and its re-appearance again may be a surviving symptom of some much larger disappearance. Quarrying plays tricks with water levels.

The sketch that I have made at the end of this chapter shows the last of the waters of Langley. After this point they plunge underground. I found by inquiring at the farm that the point of disappearance has been advanced a little upstream on account of a filling in and bridging of the hollow to take a track across to the farm but it is only a matter of a few yards. Beyond the point of disappearance is a malt-house of brick. This is built on to the road and at its side is a hollow suggestive of water which has gone.

An old man of this valley told me that he had witnessed tests intended to prove that the stream that disappeared here was the same as that which came out by Boughton Quarries. Paraffin was poured in and it is said appeared for a long time in streaks in the spring farther on, much to the indignation of people, who used this as their water supply and objected strongly to experiments made in the interest of topographical science.

Water's End, Brishing Farm.

THE SKY-LINE

I LOVE the ridge where the world leaves off
   And the roadway touches the sky,
I love to wonder what I shall find
   Across those ramparts high.
There may be a village tucked under the hill,
   Or a farm in the golden lee ;
There may be a stream and a water-mill,
   Or there may be a gleam of the sea.

OVER THE HILL

AFTER leaving Brishing Farm, which I notice in the map is marked Brishing Court, I struck out in a south-easterly direction, rather vaguely making for Headcorn. I was haunted, however, by a glimpse of a door leading into a barn which I had seen for a second or so in passing, and I retraced my steps so that I could draw it. There were two barrels and a few odd things lying about, but it made a telling subject (roughly sketched above) and is typical of so many glimpses of things one gets among these farms of the Weald—farms still yielding some of the most primitive rural scenery in England.

It often happens that the most unspoiled survivals of the countryside of any land are close to a main-line railway. Tearing through the Vosges in the Ostend-Basle express, who stops to explore the delightful recesses that one sees from the dining-car at lunch, or, bent on Brighton, what Londoner pauses to saunter through the steep glades of Balcombe Forest ? England is no exception to this strange railway protection of old corners. In the midst of the Weald of Kent, level and dead straight for twenty miles between Tonbridge and Ashford, stretches a section of line on which many trains pass but few stop. Hard by are quaint villages and timbered mansions, and all in an atmosphere of that Merrie England which the rush and industrialism of our age had threatened once to destroy, but now curiously enough, has come to preserve. For it is the very efficiency of our modern roads and modern transport that has inaugurated a new era, and the people of villages who were selling their oak timbers to enterprising furniture-makers, and regarding their legacies from the past as rather a tumbledown nuisance, are beginning to realize that they have an asset in these old-world things. Mine host of the " Woolpack " scents business, and begins to see in the motor-car what his forebears saw in Kentish broadcloth, and Old Tom, the archæologically-inclined sexton of the historic Wealden Church, reaps as good a harvest as ever the pilgrims yielded to his ancestors on their way to the shrine of Holy Thomas of Canterbury.

I often wish that we could rub into the heads of district councillors that these things are a commercial asset. The argument of an artist, I know, falls flat, but tell them " *It pays* " and we may get a following.

Some of the old farmhouses and cottages have been "discovered" by people who prize them, and they have been preserved, and, where restoration was necessary, restored with care and reverence for their ancient lineage. Mr. Lewis Hind's delightful Elizabethan cottage, Island Farm, near Biddenden, is an example of this regard for the past.

The Forest of Anderida extended from Kent through Sussex into the eastern parts of Hampshire and northwards to Surrey. Mostly dense wood, it was chequered with tracts of open heath and very sparsely populated. The Romans occupied it, drove Stane Street through it, and worked it for iron. The name Weald came with the Saxons. It has a family connexion with Wald, Wold, Wild. Lambarde defines weald as the wooded portion and wold as the bare hills rising from this. (Compare Schwarzwald, the Wolds in Lincolnshire, the Cotswolds, and the like.)

Well, to capture a little of this spacious quality of old England, this "blue goodness of the Weald" of which Kipling sings, come with me to Headcorn and stand by the old mill, a veritable cameo of Merrie England, still harnessing the winds and defying change, and I will show you a landscape such as will sweep the cobwebs from your brain, a breezy, broad and all-English landscape (not British this time, ye patriots of the North), a landscape with "no nonsense about it." The village below, with its ancient church and half-timbered vicarage, the oasthouses, those true castles of Kent, nestling in the trees—castles that defend our ancient liberties from prohibitionist invaders, and above and beyond it all—

"Belt upon belt, the wooded, dim,
Blue goodness of the weald."

This region is a fascinating one to explore, if you have the ability to read history in little things. For instance, you will note the frequency of the Woolpack Inn, speaking of days when the broadcloth of Kent was famed the world over and when caravans of loaded horses in single file traversed the otherwise impassable country by means of tracks cut through the forest. These paved narrow ways still exist, and at Biddenden and Staplehurst very good examples of them can be seen running parallel with the road.

The weavers—the first Flemish influx occurring in the reign of Edward III—brought great prosperity to these towns. The decline of the weaving industry coincided with the rise of the iron-smelting trade, which became so important a factor in the wealth of England. It is here that the cloth country gives way to the iron country. Biddenden and Tenterden are places where the two industries existed side by side.

The great days of the broadcloth of Kent were before the Elizabethan age. The most prosperous times of the furnaces, however, were at the end of that era, after which they began to decline until 1825, when the last furnace died down.

At Headcorn the main line to Folkestone and Dover stretches in a straight line. From the bridge the lines of rails can be seen stretching away on either side to the horizon. This marks dramatically the centre of the Wealden plain. On either side of this way lies level land swelling into low hills at a more or less even distance north and south. Sutton Valence and Boughton make highlands on one side, Cranbrook and Goudhurst on the other.

I am not well versed in geology, having been prevented

from studying it on account of the occultism which geologists have cast round the subject by means of nomenclature ridiculously remote from ordinary speech. As the bewildered

Springtime in the Weald

young girl exclaimed to the professor when he was trying to teach her the names of prehistoric animals: "They couldn't possibly have remembered their names themselves, so it is difficult for *us* to remember them after all these years ! " If geologists would only tell us about the formation of the world by referring to clay, chalk, sand, gravel and other familiar substances we ordinary mortals can recognize, we should get on, but I cannot struggle with neo-pleistocene-oölite and the like. Let all orthodox geologists snort and laugh in utter contempt, but I will endeavour to explain to my fellow-creatures by means of a rough diagram how I feel that the ordinary mortal could understand the formation of the Weald.

Let us imagine first a great plain of chalk some hundreds of feet deep and slightly convex as I have drawn it (page 173) the position of Headcorn being shown at A. The stratum beneath this chalk is of sandstone, known locally as rag-stone and in one place (where the quality is particularly fine for building) as Bethersden marble. This is variously " Hastings sand," gault, and " greensand " (called so by geologists because it is never green). Beneath this is a stratum of Wealden clay. For some reason (which I cannot explain) the disintegrating action of rain, frost and chemical action has " denuded " the chalk at A more rapidly than at B and C. Thus at A the chalk has entirely disappeared and the gault and " greensand " is exposed. This in turn wears down at A more rapidly than at E and F. Then the complete disappearance of this stratum exposes the Wealden clay.

The result of all this wear and tear has left the Weald of Kent, Sussex, and Surrey like a long trench running roughly east and west. In the centre are the clay lands. On each side of these are low ramparts of gault and sandstone. Each of these ridges is backed up by higher ridges of chalk land, the North Downs on one side and the South Downs (beginning at Beachy Head) on the other.

Now, as far as our march is concerned, this diagram will help to reveal the nature of the land over which we have travelled and explain that to which we are coming. At Boxley we left the chalk land of the North Downs and came to the ridge of rag-stone at Boughton. Then after many marchings and counter-marchings up and down the hill and

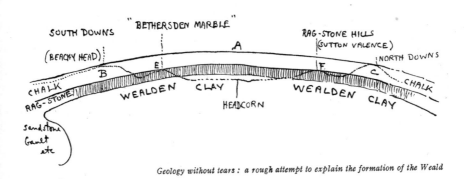

Geology without tears : a rough attempt to explain the formation of the Weald

round about this region, we struck out into the clay lands and came to Headcorn. Now as we approach Rolvenden and Tenterden the land begins to rock and swell and we are on the sandstone again and making for the sea. The ridge of chalk corresponding to the North Downs is gone, for the sea has washed it away. Westward, however, we shall find it suddenly at Beachy Head.

Lector. This is all very interesting, but I must confess I am getting a little mixed as to our itinerary.   Where exactly is the course of our road ?

Pictor.   My dear Lector, I have not the least idea.   But you will have learned by now, for you have been a faithful *compagnon de voyage*, that the Enchanted Road leads everywhere and that it never ends.

PRINTED BY
JARROLD AND SONS LTD.
NORWICH